THEN & NOW

MURFREESBORO

OPPOSITE: This picture of the north side of the public square was taken on "Cotton Day," a yearly harvesttime event, during the mid-1920s. (Courtesy Rutherford County Archives, Shacklett Historic Images Collection.)

THEN & NOW

MURFREESBORO

Bill Shacklett and John Lodl

Bill would like to dedicate this book to all of his family, particularly his father and mother, Dick and Ginny Shacklett.
John would like to dedicate this book to his wife, Jennifer, and his son, Pierce, for all their love and support.

Copyright © 2012 by Bill Shacklett and John Lodl
ISBN 978-0-7385-9111-4

Library of Congress Control Number: 2011933258

Published by Arcadia Publishing
Charleston, South Carolina

Printed in the United States of America

For all general information, please contact Arcadia Publishing:
Telephone 843-853-2070
Fax 843-853-0044
E-mail sales@arcadiapublishing.com
For customer service and orders:
Toll-Free 1-888-313-2665

Visit us on the Internet at www.arcadiapublishing.com

ON THE FRONT COVER: The Rutherford County Courthouse was constructed in 1859. This picture of the west side of the courthouse was taken around 1950. Today, the old courthouse is one of only six pre–Civil War courthouses still standing in Tennessee. (Then, courtesy Rutherford County Archives, Shacklett Historic Images Collection; Now, photograph by Bill Shacklett.)

ON THE BACK COVER: The Carnation Milk Company opened a new factory in Murfreesboro in 1927. The opening of the factory was celebrated with one of the grandest parades in Murfreesboro's history. This picture was taken of that parade on the square at the corner of East Main and Church Streets. (Courtesy Rutherford County Archives, Shacklett Historic Images Collection.)

CONTENTS

ACKNOWLEDGMENTS

The research required to answer the "who, where, and when" questions for every picture presented in this book could not be found in one location. For that reason, there are many persons for whom we owe much gratitude.

We thank Gloria Shacklett Christy for telling us the history behind many of the photographs taken by her father, especially the ones that Bill could not remember.

There are many local historians who share a common interest in preserving the history and heritage of this great place. We turned to these people for answers about our past. These people included the following: William "Bill" Ledbetter, Barry Lamb, Jim Laughlin, Bill Jakes, Toby Fancis, Don Detwiler, and Denise Carlton. We also thank Ernie Johns for sharing his knowledge on the history of Smyrna and Mike Smith for providing the history of Powell's Chapel Baptist Church. We gratefully appreciate Shelby Hunton for taking Bill up in his plane for the aerial images.

Finally, there are several organizations in town that also opened their doors for our inquiries. We thank Dr. Carroll Van West and his fine staff at the Heritage Center of Murfreesboro/Rutherford County; Rita Shacklett and her staff at the Linebaugh Library; Dr. Jim Williams and Jim Havron at the Albert Gore Research Center at Middle Tennessee State University (MTSU); Anita Teague and staff at the Sam Davis Home; James Manning and staff at Oaklands Historic House Museum; the staff of Bradley Academy Museum & Cultural Center; the staff at Jennings and Ayers Funeral Home; the staff at St. Mark's United Methodist Church; and Gib Backlund, Jim Lewis, John George, and all the great staff at Stones River National Battlefield.

To make this book a truly sentimental journey, we matched Then photographs taken by the late Richard Shacklett with Now photographs taken by his son Bill Shacklett. Therefore, unless otherwise noted, all of the historical images in this book are courtesy of the Shacklett Historic Images Collection, currently housed at the Rutherford County Archives. These rare images of Murfreesboro and Rutherford County were either originally taken by Dick Shacklett or they were older images restored by him in his photography studio. Unless otherwise noted, the Now photographs were taken by Bill Shacklett.

Last but not least, we thank the Read To Succeed program of Rutherford County. This nonprofit initiative supports literacy programs in our county. The authors' proceeds from the sale of this book will go to support Read To Succeed's mission.

INTRODUCTION

Founded in 1803, Rutherford County, Tennessee, runs deep with history and heritage. The city of Murfreesboro was founded as the county seat in 1811 and retains the distinction of being the exact geographic center of the entire state. For that reason, Murfreesboro served as the state capital of Tennessee from 1818 until 1826. Murfreesboro and Rutherford County also hold the distinction of serving as the focal point for one of the greatest Civil War conflicts, the Battle of Stones River.

Murfreesboro has one of only six pre–Civil War courthouses still standing in Tennessee. Three times in its history, the courthouse faced destruction to make room for modern government facilities. The first occurrence took place during the Great Depression in the 1930s, but federal assistance money simply dried up before the demolition plans could be finalized. On two other occasions, once in the late 1950s and again in the 1970s, plans to replace the old courthouse were derailed by local citizens driven by the plea of historic preservation. Through it all, Murfreesboro has managed to retain not only the historic courthouse, but also most of the historic buildings on the square. Since the late 1980s, the Murfreesboro Main Street program has revitalized the historic downtown area and brought renewed interest to this part of town.

However, while Murfreesboro fought to retain much of its historic character, preservation efforts around the city and county battled with developers as Rutherford County boomed during the latest housing explosion in this country. So, there is much to compare between what was here "then" and what is here "now." These complexities between preservation and development make Murfreesboro one of the most unique places in the country: with strong ties to history, but always looking to the future.

During his lifetime, Richard "Dick" Shacklett captured much of the history of Murfreesboro through his camera. Shacklett took a job as a photographer's apprentice while in high school in the 1930s. After serving in World War II, he returned to Murfreesboro and opened his own studio, Shacklett's Photography, which he operated until his death in 1994. After his passing, Richard's children, Bill and Gloria, took over the family business that is still in operation today. In 2010, the Shacklett family donated over 30,000 historical images taken by Dick Shacklett to the Rutherford County Archives to be preserved and presented to the public.

In addition to the thousands of pictures taken by Dick Shacklett, the Shacklett Historic Images Collection also contains restoration negatives, also known as "copy negatives," that he took while restoring older photographs for customers. Altogether, these negatives and photographs represent one of the largest collections of historical images in the state of Tennessee and record the history of Murfreesboro and Rutherford County from roughly the 1860s to the 1980s. Although some of these images have been depicted in previous publications, there are thousands more that have been kept from the public eye until now. This book will serve as a showcase for the Shacklett Historic Images Collection.

CHAPTER

DOWNTOWN AND
AROUND THE SQUARE

The Rutherford County Courthouse is one of only six pre–Civil War courthouses still standing in Tennessee. Originally constructed in 1859, the courthouse has undergone two major alterations.

This picture was taken looking west from the end of East Main Street around 1880. Today, the courthouse is an integral part of Rutherford County's past, present, and future.

The first major renovation to the courthouse took place between 1907 and 1908. The roof was changed from a hip roof to a flat roof, and the cupola was replaced. This provided additional space inside the building to lower the second floor and add a third floor. Finally, entrances were added on the north and south sides of the building, while the main entrances on the east and west sides were widened.

The last major alteration to the exterior of the courthouse took place in 1960 when the two-story wings were added to the north and south ends. This expansion provided desperately needed new office space for the growing county government. This was an era when almost all of the county offices were still located within the old courthouse. The sign for the James K. Polk Hotel is clearly visible in this 1960s photograph.

The courthouse came close to destruction on three different occasions in the 1900s. In 1937, the county court and local citizens deemed that renovations to the "old building" would be too costly. However, America's involvement in World War II stalled the demolition plans. In 1959, local citizens convinced the county court to remodel the building once again, instead of replacing it. Finally, in the late 1970s, the county court again needed additional space. This time, a new judicial building was constructed.

The Confederate monument stands as one of the most historic remembrances to the War Between the States, also known as the American Civil War. The monument was constructed in 1900 and originally faced toward East Main Street. The monument was moved to the northeast corner of the courthouse lawn in 1914. This rare image shows the monument in its original location. Over the years, additional monuments have been constructed around the square to remind citizens of fallen veterans from many wars.

In 1927, the Carnation Milk Company bought the former Lytle family plantation just west of the square and constructed a large plant. The dedication of this new venture was celebrated around the square with a grand parade and a barbecue feast.

This picture was taken from East Main Street looking toward the courthouse. Notice the sign on the side of the building for A.L. Smith & Company, which used to be a locally famous pharmacy.

The town of Murfreesboro was established in 1811 when county officials decided to move their seat of government from the old town of Jefferson to a more central location. The land for the new town was donated by William Lytle and was named Murfreesboro in honor of Col. Hardy Murfree. Lytle did not realize that part of the land he donated actually belonged to the Murfree family. But once the error was confirmed, the Murfree family graciously relinquished its rights to the south side of the square in 1818. (Now, courtesy John Lodl.)

Although Murfreesboro's historic square witnessed fires, the Civil War, and even a tornado, it still retains much of its character and history. This picture was taken in the mid-1920s when local farmers used to bring their cotton crops to market on the square. Today, much of the maintenance and upkeep of the square and buildings falls under the guidance of Main Street Murfreesboro/Rutherford County Inc.

This picture of the Murfreesboro Battery Service Station was taken in 1934. The service station opened sometime before 1925 at the corner of East College Street and North Maple Street. Many older residents remember when the building was occupied by the Sue & Willie Service Station and Restaurant. Rutherford County government acquired the structure in the early 1980s, and it now houses part of the county courts. Notice the marquee for the Princess Theatre to the left in the older photograph.

The First Baptist Church was organized in Murfreesboro in 1843. The congregation moved to the corner of East Main and South Church Streets in 1891. In 1919, members decided to construct the current building, which was completed in 1920. Ironically, the Baptist congregation was forced to the sell the church during the Great Depression, but it was able to buy it back in 1941. The house to the left of the church in this picture was the parsonage, which was constructed in 1915.

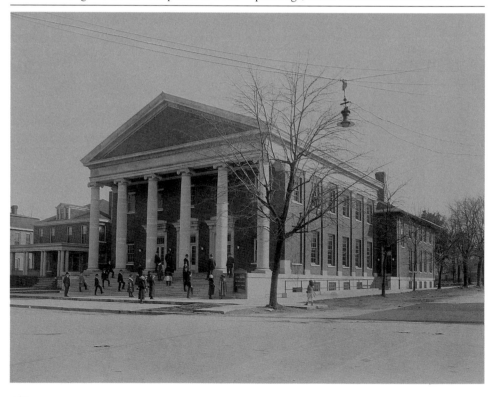

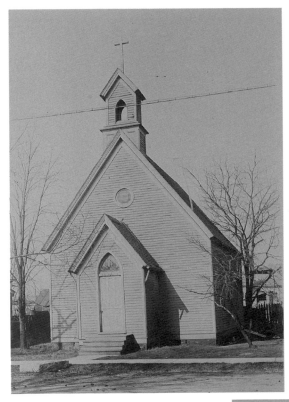

St. Paul's Episcopal Church was originally constructed on Spring Street in 1897. The building was moved in 1926 to its present location facing East Main Street. At the same time, the outside of the building was covered with stone veneer. This picture was taken in the early 1900s when the church was still located on Spring Street. The congregation expanded its facilities in the early 2000s, and now St. Paul's is one of the premier churches on historic East Main Street.

In 1913, a tornado tore through downtown Murfreesboro causing destruction to many buildings on and around the square. This picture of the First Presbyterian Church shows that the original bell tower and roof were literally blown away, while the rest of the building remained in place. The congregation decided to salvage the majority of the building; however, they did alter the front of the building and added a domed roof. (Now, courtesy John Lodl.)

Construction of the old Methodist church building at the corner of Church Street and College Street began in 1886 and was completed in 1888. The church witnessed many additions as the congregation grew in the 1900s. In 2003, the First United Methodist congregation moved to West Thompson Lane. The old church building became the new main office for MidSouth Bank of Murfreesboro. Today, MidSouth Bank is one of the premier local banks in Murfreesboro and takes pride in its historic building.

The Spur Gas Station was built on the corner of North Spring Street and East College Street in the late 1940s. The property changed ownership in 1978 and underwent major renovations. The center of the original gas station was retained for office space, while the left and right wings were demolished. Another building was also constructed in front of the old gas station to provide additional office space. Today, an Edward Jones investment company office occupies the original building.

The first passenger train arrived in Murfreesboro on July 4, 1851. The occasion was marked with a grand celebration and barbecue feast hosted by the citizens of the town. To accommodate the increase in railroad transportation after the Civil War, a new train depot was built in 1887. This picture from the 1940s shows passengers waiting for the next train. Today, the train depot is owned by CSX Corporation Inc. as part of its railroad operations.

In 1936, Edwin Ayers moved the Jennings and Ayers Funeral Home from Cainsville, Tennessee, to Murfreesboro. The funeral home occupied a few different locations close to the square until 1963, when Edwin Ayers purchased the old Ledbetter family home at 820 South Church Street and had it remodeled to suit his business. This snowy scene was taken around 1966. Church Street was just a two-lane road back then, so the front yard was much wider than it is today.

In the 1950s, an actor from California visited Murfreesboro to formally announce that General Electric was about to break ground for a new factory. That actor, Ronald Reagan, later became the 40th president of the United States. The General Electric plant opened for operation in Murfreesboro in 1957. For nearly 50 years, the plant manufactured electric motors for clothes washers and dryers and employed hundreds of Rutherford County workers. The plant closed in November 2006, and the site's future is unclear.

In 1929, Middle Tennessee State University (MTSU) and Rutherford County government collaborated to build a new training school across the street from the main university campus. The school opened its doors in January 1929. In 1985, the school was officially renamed the Homer Pittard Campus School in honor of the local educator and historian. This rare photograph shows the construction of the training school the year before it opened. (Now, courtesy John Lodl.)

McFadden School has served the educational needs of Murfreesboro's children since it opened in 1927. However, the school was plagued with numerous fires in its early years. One of the worst fires—depicted in this rare photograph—occurred on Sunday, January 26, 1939. However, the school was rebuilt that same year using the architectural plans from the previous building. Today, the building houses one of the Murfreesboro City Schools' magnet programs. (Now, courtesy John Lodl.)

Holloway High School was constructed in 1929 to serve the needs of African American students in Murfreesboro and the surrounding area. In 1954, a gymnasium and new wing with five additional classrooms were added to the original structure. The school was closed in 1968 during the integration of the local schools. The original portion of the Holloway facilities was razed in the 1980s; however, the gymnasium and the 1954 classroom addition are utilized today by the Rutherford County School system.

Oaklands Mansion, which was constructed in the 1800s, remained one of Murfreesboro's most elegant residences well into the 1900s. However, the home became vacant in the 1950s. In 1958, the City of Murfreesboro purchased the property for a park and housing development. A group of local women petitioned the city to save the old home. This picture was taken in 1959, just prior to the restoration of the house. Today, Oaklands Mansion is the only historic home open for public tours in Murfreesboro.

The General Assembly of the State of Tennessee passed an act in 1909 to establish four normal schools for the training of schoolteachers in the state. Murfreesboro won the bid for the school that would be located in the mid-state region. Middle Tennessee Normal, as it was then called, open its doors in September 1911. Today, Middle Tennessee State University has the largest undergraduate student population in the entire state. This picture shows the Kirksey Old Main Building in the 1920s.

The Alumni Memorial Gym was constructed on MTSU's campus in 1950 as a tribute to all the university's alumni who lost their lives in World War II. In addition to the modern gymnasium, the building housed all the sports and recreation programs and served as the principal venue for graduations for many years. Today, there is a memorial wall on campus that lists all the names of alumni who have lost their lives defending the country.

A new post office building was constructed in Murfreesboro in 1909 at the corner of North Church and College Streets. This picture was taken in the mid-1920s. The US government operated the Murfreesboro Post Office in this building for over 50 years. The City of Murfreesboro acquired the building in 1962, and it became the new location for Linebaugh Library. In 1992, the library moved to the new Murfreesboro City Plaza, and the Center for the Arts took over the building.

CHAPTER 2

OUT IN THE COUNTY

Construction on the original turnpike linking Murfreesboro to Nashville was started in 1832 and completed in 1842. By the early 1900s, when this picture was taken, the Murfreesboro-to-Nashville turnpike was part of the Dixie Highway. Redoubt Brannan, part of a Union fort, is visible in the top center of the picture.

It is thought that the dam site at Walter Hill has been in existence since the formation of Rutherford County in 1803. Originally, the dam provided power for a mill, but sometime around 1905, it began producing electricity as part of the City Gas and Electric Light Company. The dam facility was purchased by the Tennessee Electric Power Company (TEPCO) in 1926 and was later sold to the City of Murfreesboro. Today, the dam still serves as a great fishing hole.

The Murfreesboro Municipal Airport grew out of the airport training facilities that started on MTSU's campus in the early 1940s. The airport was dedicated in 1952 to serve the needs of local citizens as well as aviation students from the university. This picture shows the airport as it appeared in the 1960s. Today, the airport is operated by the City of Murfreesboro. Its largest tenant, the MTSU Department of Aerospace, is ranked in the top five aviation programs in the country.

The veterans hospital opened on the outskirts of Murfreesboro in January 1940 with 15 buildings and the ability to house 600 patients. By the 1960s, the hospital had grown to accommodate over 1,500 patients. In 1984, the hospital was renamed in honor of Sgt. Alvin C. York, a veteran and hero of World War I. Today, the Alvin C. York Campus is an integral part of the federal Veterans Health Administration in the state of Tennessee.

The Bethel Methodist Church is located on Sulphur Springs Road in the Bethel community, northwest of Murfreesboro. The current structure was built in 1887 to replace the previous church, which was constructed in the early 1800s, to serve the community. The Bethel Schoolhouse was still in use when this picture was taken around 1940. The Shacklett family attended this church whenever they visited the family farm near the Bethel community.

Powell's Chapel Baptist Church started in 1875 on land donated by the Malone family in the northern section of the county. Members named the church after their first pastor, Dr. W.D. Powell. When the original church burned in 1929, a new building was constructed. This picture was taken around 1939, after the congregation voted to buy a church bus. Today, Powell's Chapel Church is still thriving and represents one of the oldest churches in the county.

The Sam Davis Home in Smyrna represents a typical Tennessee "I" house with its main central hallway flanked by rooms on either side. The home was acquired by the State of Tennessee in 1927 to serve as a memorial to Sam Davis, a Confederate war hero who gave his life for his country during the American Civil War. The site has been in continuous operation as a museum since 1930 under the stewardship of the Sam Davis Memorial Association.

This house is known as the Sam Davis Boyhood Home. This house was originally located in the vicinity of Almaville Road and Interstate 24 in Smyrna. Sam was born in this home in 1842 and lived there for eight years before his father purchased the larger estate where the Sam Davis Home & Museum are located today. The boyhood home was moved to the museum property in 1974, shortly after this picture was taken.

The Bank of Smyrna opened in 1904 and was the first bank located in the small town. The name changed to the Peoples Bank of Smyrna by 1908. A new building was constructed in 1910, and the name was changed to First National Bank the following year, which was when this picture was taken. The building lost its front columns when Lowry Street became part of the New Nashville Highway (Highway US 41) in the 1950s.

The town now known as Eagleville began around 1800 as a stop on the stagecoach line running between Nashville and Shelbyville. The name Eagleville was adopted in 1836 when the town received its first post office. This picture was taken about 1950 looking north on Main Street where it crosses Highway 99. Not much has changed in the little town of Eagleville over the years.

AN AERIAL VIEW OF RUTHERFORD COUNTY

Murfreesboro has witnessed many changes over the years, yet the town retains much of its history. The county courthouse was central to the formation of the city from the early days of settlement and continues to be the center of the community today. This photograph was taken around 1970.

This c. 1940 aerial photograph of downtown Murfreesboro shows the town in the era just before urban renewal. The main road into town was the Dixie Highway, or West College Street, as seen at the top of this photograph. And in a time before fast-food restaurants and shopping malls, every convenience centered around the downtown square. In the 1950s, the creation of the Broad Street Project would forever change the landscape of Murfreesboro.

AN AERIAL VIEW OF RUTHERFORD COUNTY

In 1905, the Baptist State Convention of Tennessee created an educational committee to establish a college for women. The committee settled on the former Union University campus on East Main Street in Murfreesboro. The new building was completed and ready for occupation by September 1907. The Tennessee College for Women survived for almost 40 years before being dissolved in 1945. The school was merged with Cumberland University in Lebanon, Tennessee. Today, this site is the location of Central Magnet School.

This aerial photograph of MTSU was taken between 1940 and 1941 when there were relatively few buildings on the campus. These structures include the main academic building, the cafeteria, the Murfree Library, a science building, and three dormitories. The university witnessed massive growth in the years following World War II. Almost all of the buildings depicted in this picture are still standing today.

This 1970s photograph shows the intersection of Mercury Boulevard and East Main Street toward the back of the MTSU campus looking west. Most of this "green space" has been covered by an ever-growing college campus. The family-housing dormitories were the only buildings to the rear of the campus in the 1970s. Today, those dormitories are in the middle of a campus that stretches from East Main Street to Greenland Drive and from Middle Tennessee Boulevard to Rutherford Boulevard.

This photograph shows the intersection of Memorial Boulevard and Broad Street in the 1970s. This picture reflects a time before the construction of Old Fort Parkway and the development of Stones River Mall. The old Carnation Milk plant is visible in the lower left corner. Today, this intersection is one of the busiest in the county. The only reminder of the old milk plant is the towering smokestack that is still standing.

AN AERIAL VIEW OF RUTHERFORD COUNTY

This 1960s aerial photograph shows the "triangle" created by Broad Street, Memorial Boulevard, and Lokey Lane (today's Medical Center Parkway). The Chromolox factory is in the center of the photograph. The Grantland Rice baseball field can be seen on the other side of Memorial Boulevard from the factory. Jackson Heights Plaza on Broad Street was a major hub of activity in the years before the development of the shopping malls.

This aerial from the 1960s shows Todd Lake, which is located between Manchester Highway and Bradyville Pike. In the 1920s and 1930s, Todd Lake was a favorite recreation center for local citizens. This part of town became prime real estate in the years after World War II as Murfreesboro saw the same housing boom as the rest of the country. Today, there are no public access points to Todd Lake, which has been surrounded by modern residential development.

AN AERIAL VIEW OF RUTHERFORD COUNTY

This aerial photograph from the 1950s was taken looking south toward the Murfreesboro airport and downtown Murfreesboro. Before the recent economic downturn, Rutherford County was an area of booming development and the 20th-fastest-growing county in the nation. The contrast between these two photographs is evidence of that growth. Today, Rutherford County is home to new economic opportunities, but also prides itself on heritage tourism.

The Alvin C. York Veterans Hospital opened on January 1, 1940, about five miles north of downtown Murfreesboro. This aerial from the 1950s shows the large campus. Over the past few decades, this area of the county has witnessed much development, and the hospital lies right on the edge of the new city limits of Murfreesboro. The large "hill" in the top center of the modern photograph is the landfill, which has also been growing over the past few decades.

VANISHING SCENES
ON THE LANDSCAPE

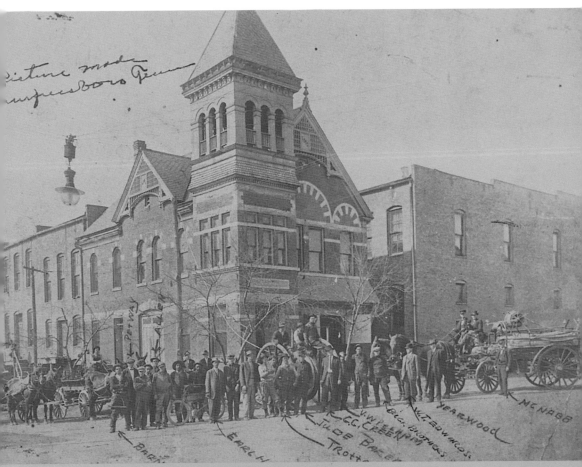

The Murfreesboro City Hall has occupied many locations throughout the years. This picture was taken in 1913 when the city hall shared a building with the fire hall at the corner of Vine and Church Streets. City hall moved from this location in 1928, and the structure was razed in 1935 to expand the rear of the Goldstein Building.

After acquiring the old Cumberland Presbyterian Church in 1928, the city used this location as the city hall until 1957. This picture was taken on July 7, 1957, the day that the building was auctioned by the city. It was purchased by the National Bank of Murfreesboro and razed to make way for a modern structure. The James K. Polk Hotel can be seen in the background, where the SunTrust Bank Building stands today.

The Jordan Hotel on East Main Street actually started out as the Ready family home, which was constructed in the 1840s. This house witnessed the famous wedding between Mattie Ready and Confederate general John Hunt Morgan during the Civil War. In 1885, the old home was purchased by Edward Leland Jordan and converted into the Jordan Hotel by adding a third floor and a new facade. The building was razed in the summer of 1965 to make way for a new bank.

One of the most famous landmarks on East Main Street during the 1900s was the James K. Polk Hotel. The business opened in March 1929 as Murfreesboro's newest upscale hotel. While Dick Shacklett was still attending high school, he opened his first photography studio in the hotel in 1938. The hotel closed in the late 1970s, and the building was razed in 1977 to make way for the modern SunTrust Bank Building, which still occupies the site today.

VANISHING SCENES ON THE LANDSCAPE

Joe Murray's Gas Station was located on the corner of East Main and Academy Streets from 1960 until 1977. Due to its location, this business was purchased along with the James K. Polk Hotel to make way for a modern bank building. Today, a parking lot is located on the former gas station location to serve the customers of SunTrust Bank.

After meeting in several locations during the early to mid-1800s, the Church of Christ denomination in Murfreesboro purchased the lot at the corner of East Main and Academy Streets in 1859. The church constructed a new brick house of worship that same year. The building was used as a post chapel by the Union army during the Civil War. This picture of the church was taken in the 1880s. In 1900, the Church of Christ was razed and replaced with a newer structure by the congregation.

Princess Theatre was originally opened on the square around 1914 by the Crescent Amusement Company but moved to the corner of North Maple and College Streets in the mid-1920s. The Princess Theatre was a huge center of entertainment in Murfreesboro—especially before the advent of television. The theater remained in operation until the early 1970s and was eventually razed. Today, the site is occupied by the Pinnacle Bank Building.

Once located at the corner of Maple and College Streets was the Haynes Hotel, as seen in this 1930s photograph. The hotel opened in 1904 and remained in operation until 1956. Adjacent to the hotel and fronting Maple Street was a bus station and garage built by James Cason sometime before 1920. These two historic landmarks were demolished in the 1950s to make way for the J.C. Penney store. Today, this site is occupied by the Pinnacle Bank Building.

VANISHING SCENES ON THE LANDSCAPE

The J.C. Penney store originally opened on the square in Murfreesboro in the early 1920s. Having outgrown that space by the 1950s, the retailer acquired the lot on the corner of West College Street and North Maple Street where the Haynes Hotel was located. The new store opened about 1958 and remained there until 1983. Today, the Miller and Lowry Building occupies the former location of this structure.

From about 1850 until the 1920s, a large carriage-manufacturing business was located on the southwest corner of West Main and Walnut Streets. After the old factory was demolished, Allen's Service Station occupied the corner lot from the 1920s until the early 1960s. Today, this location is the site of a newer building housing offices for First State Finance and Tennessee state representative Diane Black.

The old county jail building, depicted in this early 1960s photograph, was constructed in 1887 at the corner of West Main and Front Streets. This building was razed around 1961 and replaced with a modern jail. By 1998, the county had outgrown the newer building and moved to a new campus on Salem Pike (US Highway 99). The old jail lot at the corner of West Main Street and Front Street is now vacant.

Before the passage of the National Interstate and Defense Highways Act of 1956 by President Eisenhower, the old Dixie Highway (US 41) was the main transportation route through Rutherford County. Automobile service stations, like the Six-Eight Tire Co. and Sinclair, depicted in this c. 1940 photograph, popped up all along the route to service travelers. The Six-Eight station is long gone, but the Sinclair Building can still be seen at the corner of South Maney Avenue and Southeast Broad Street.

Under the Federal Housing Act of 1949, the City of Murfreesboro gained federal assistance to build new urban housing projects and to vacate the residents living in an old section of Murfreesboro called The Bottoms. Locally, this program was called the Broad Street Project because it rerouted State Route 41 (Nashville Highway) southwest of the courthouse and directly through The Bottoms. This new section of the highway would be called Broad Street.

The Bottoms was located southwest of the courthouse between West Main Street and South Church Street. This low-lying area would flood every spring when Lytle Creek overflowed its banks. However, this area was also the center of a historic African American community that traced it roots to the ending of the Civil War. By the time this picture was taken in the early 1950s, the dated and dilapidated houses were deemed a blighted area for Murfreesboro.

After the creation of Broad Street in the 1950s, the area between West Main Street and South Maney Avenue on the new highway became heavily commercialized. Patterson's Food Market was located at 306 Southeast Broad Street from 1964 through 1968. This later became the location for Arthur's Bi-Rite from 1969 through 1981. Today, Road Runners pawn shop is located at this address, which is where South Academy Street intersects with Broad Street.

By the early 1900s, South Church Street was occupied by residential houses and commercial enterprises, like the Sunshine Hosiery Mill. But during 1950s, this area was engulfed by urban renewal projects. The Dixie Furniture store moved to 313 South Church Street in 1969, about the same time that this picture was taken. The store remained in business here until 1987. Shortly thereafter, South Church Street witnessed the construction of the modern Murfreesboro Civic Plaza on one side and Murfreesboro's first and only skyscraper, the NHC Building, on the other.

Charles Burton Ragland Sr. moved to Murfreesboro in the early 1900s and started Ragland, Potter & Co. around 1917. Ragland later moved to Nashville and expanded his wholesale grocery business, which serviced most of the Southeast. This picture was taken around 1922 when the Ragland, Potter & Co. warehouse was located at 208 South Front Street in Murfreesboro. Today, this site is occupied by Sticks and Stuff Furniture Store on the corner of Broad Street and South Front Street.

DeJarnett and McCullough Live Stock Exchange opened for business near the corner of West Castle Street and South Walnut Street around 1918. J.W. Donnell & Sons acquired the stockyard in 1922, about the time that this picture was taken, and remained in business well into the 1940s. Today, it is hard to image livestock roaming the streets in front of the Home Building Products Inc., which is located on this site.

VANISHING SCENES ON THE LANDSCAPE

In 1809, Bradley Academy became one of the first schools formed in the new county of Rutherford. In the 1830s, Bradley Academy moved into a new brick building on Academy Street, as depicted in this Civil War–era picture of the school. In 1884, the Bradley Academy building was authorized to be used for the education of African Americans. The pre–Civil War building was razed in 1917 to construct a newer school. Today, the 1917 building is operated as the Bradley Academy Museum and Cultural Center.

In 1848, the Baptists of Middle Tennessee laid the cornerstone for a school on East Main Street. Construction of the new building, called Union University, was completed in 1853. Union University was highly successful before the Civil War but sustained extensive physical and financial damage during the war. Union University was moved to Jackson, Tennessee, in 1874. This site was later used for the Tennessee College for Women and is the location for today's Central Magnet School.

Before the integration of schools in Murfreesboro, Central High School served the white students of the town. In September 1919, the school moved into a new brick building on North Maple Street where the Murfreesboro Housing Authority is located today. The school was highly modern, with 16 classrooms, a large gymnasium, and "bubbling sanitary drinking fountains." This picture shows the fire that destroyed the Central High School building on March 30, 1944. After the fire, the school reopened on East Main Street.

The Rutherford County Hospital, which opened in May 1927, was constructed as part of a five-year rural health initiative organized by the Commonwealth Fund of New York. This picture was taken c. 1950. The name of the hospital was changed to Middle Tennessee Medical Center Inc. in 1982. The old hospital was officially closed in October 2010 when MTMC moved to a new facility on Medical Center Parkway. As of this writing, the old hospital is being razed.

VANISHING SCENES ON THE LANDSCAPE

On the south side of the 1000 block of East Main Street was the Mooney School for Boys, which was constructed in 1901. The locally famous Kerr Athletic Field was located adjacent to the school, as seen in this 1920s photograph. The Mooney School was demolished in the late 1930s, and the entire block was subdivided for modern housing. Only one small vacant lot remains of the once famous ball field. (Now, courtesy John Lodl.)

St. Mark's United
Methodist Church
originated in a
renovated dairy barn
on North Tennessee
Boulevard on August
6, 1930. By 1951,
the congregation had
outgrown the old barn
as well as a second
sanctuary, so a new
church was constructed
on East Main Street.
This snowy scene was
photographed in 1966.
The congregation
expanded into a larger
campus on Rutherford
Boulevard in 2002,
and the church on East
Main Street was razed
and replaced with a
parking lot for MTSU.

The old Rutherford County Fairgrounds were once located on South Church Street. The fairgrounds opened in 1868 when a private company of gentlemen purchased 20 acres of land and established a half-mile racetrack, an amphitheater, animal stalls, and numerous other buildings. The fairgrounds had varying success under different proprietors for many decades lasting well into the 1900s. Today, modern development is slowly encroaching upon the site.

The Stones River National Cemetery was established in 1865 for the burial of Union soldiers. The original cemetery superintendent's house, shown here, was constructed in 1871. That building was razed around 1920 and replaced with a more modern structure. Neither of the houses remains today, but a reconstructed bandstand rises close to the original site. Today, the cemetery is part of the Stones River National Battlefield, which is operated by the National Park Service.

This picture of the Manson Pike Bridge over Overall's Creek was taken in 1884. This bridge provided a main thoroughfare to and from Murfreesboro during the Battle of Stones River. This bridge saw major action between December 31, 1862, and January 2, 1863, when over 81,000 Confederate and Union soldiers met on the battlefield near Murfreesboro. Today, this area is being heavily developed as the commercial district of Murfreesboro continues to move away from the historic downtown area and out to the interstate. (Now, courtesy John Lodl.)

VANISHING SCENES ON THE LANDSCAPE

In 1890, several businessmen obtained a charter of incorporation to start the Murfreesboro Water Works Company. This private firm erected a pumping station and reservoir at Murfree's Spring. The company had the sole right to furnish clean drinking water to the citizens and businesses of Murfreesboro. Today, the site that once housed the first water pumping station for Murfreesboro lies in the wetland preserve behind the children's museum, better known as the Discovery Center at Murfree's Spring.

Ransom Mill was located on the West Fork of Stones River near the present-day intersection of Medical Center Parkway and Old Nashville Highway. A mill was originally constructed on this site in the early 1800s by David Dickinson, who married Fanny Noialles Murfree, daughter of Col. Hardy Murfree. Today, the mill is long gone, but the dam provides a favorite fishing spot on Murfreesboro's Greenway System, a series of urban trails in the heart of the city.

Located about a half mile north of the Halls Hill community on the north bank of the east branch of Stones River, the Halls Hill Mill was built around 1850. The mill was dismantled in 1879 and moved to the opposite side of the Stones River. It was destroyed by a flood in 1902 but was quickly rebuilt. The mill remained in operation until the 1940s and was demolished around 1978. Today, the site serves as a great watering hole for horses.

VANISHING SCENES ON THE LANDSCAPE

B5963   Depot, Christiana, Tenn.

The village of Christiana was founded in the 1850s as a railroad stop along the Nashville-Chattanooga line south of Murfreesboro. The train depot depicted in this picture was built in 1882 and was the second such structure to serve the village. This building remained in service until 1942. Today, only a post office, restaurant, gift shop, and a few old houses remain in Christiana. (Now, courtesy John Lodl.)

Fat Gambill's garage was once located at the intersection of Highway 102 and the Dixie Highway in the Hilltop community. Hilltop was an African American enclave with houses, churches, and a high school. Today, that intersection is known as Enon Springs Road and Old Nashville Highway in the town of Smyrna. Although the gas station is long gone, the land where it sat was not paved over with the widening of Old Nashville Highway a few years ago.

The town of Smyrna was founded in the mid-1800s as a railroad stop between Nashville and Murfreesboro. In 1869, the town was incorporated and became a hub of local activity. In the 1950s, the construction of New Nashville Highway (US 41) would pass through the middle of Smyrna on top of Lowry Street and forever change the "small-town" feel of the village.

The earliest known general store in Smyrna was opened prior to the Civil War by Maj. Houston Dudley. In 1885, the store was purchased by the Jarratt brothers, Dudley and Will. In 1908, the business became known as Jarratt & McColloch.

The store went out of business in the late 1920s, and the building burned around 1930. Today, this location is owned by the City of Smyrna and is used as a public parking lot.

VANISHING SCENES ON THE LANDSCAPE

The Rutherford Motor Company opened its doors at 108 South Front Street in Smyrna in 1922. Ford Model T automobiles as well as Ford tractors were delivered by train and sold at the shop. The business closed in 1928, and the building burned in 1931. The two larger buildings adjacent to the old car dealership are still standing in historic downtown Smyrna.

This picture was taken from Lowry Street looking down Madison Street (today's Sam Hager Street) in 1920. The wagons full of cotton were on their way to S.E. Hager's cotton gin. The front of the Smyrna First United Methodist Church building can be seen in the extreme upper right. Today, Smyrna is home to a Nissan automotive factory and part of a thriving community.

One of the most productive cotton gins in Rutherford County was the Hager Gin in Smyrna. S.E. Hager built the gin in 1882, and it stayed in operation until the late 1920s. This picture was taken around 1915 with the gin in full production. Today, the gin site is covered by a modern gas station on Lowry Street.

A gentleman by the name of E.E. Nance moved to Smyrna in 1918 and opened a red-cedar yard on Hazelwood Drive. Nance moved the lumberyard to Madison Street (present-day Sam Hager Street) in the 1920s, which was about when this picture was taken. Today, part of this site serves as a parking lot for the Smyrna First United Methodist Church.

VANISHING SCENES ON THE LANDSCAPE

This bridge stretched over the west fork of the Stones River leading into the town of Jefferson, as depicted in this 1920s photograph. Jefferson was founded around 1803 and served as the first center of government for Rutherford County from 1804 until Murfreesboro was founded in 1811. Jefferson was a thriving hub of activity when the Stones River was still the major artery of transportation for the county. However, with the advent of the railroad by the mid-1800s, Jefferson became less viable. (Now, courtesy John Lodl.)

In the 1960s, the federal government purchased all of the property in and around Jefferson as part of the J. Percy Priest Lake Project, which placed a dam on the Stones River to provide electricity. The Jefferson School and all the other buildings of the town were razed. This picture of Jefferson School was taken around 1940. However, the land where the town was located did not flood. Today, this area is part of the US Army Corps of Engineers property and is accessible by hiking trails. (Now, courtesy John Lodl.)

Jefferson Springs was a resort area located about a mile north of Jefferson. The sulphur spring for which the area was named is said to have been discovered in the mid-1800s and was located in the river channel. The area quickly grew into a resort town with hotels, cottages, restaurants, stores, and private residences. The bridge was dynamited in 1967, and the buildings razed to make way for the J. Percy Priest Lake Project.

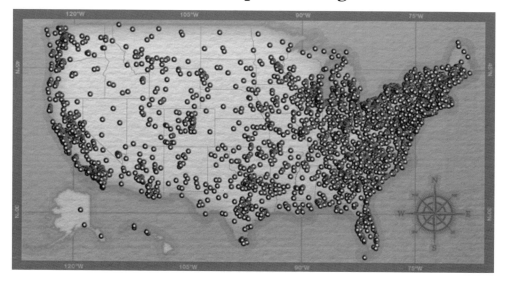